My first

Written by
Tapasi De

Illustrated by
Suman S. Roy

Dad bought a pet.

It's a puppy.

It's brown in colour.

It's furry too.

We named it Ginger.

He is very small.

Ginger sleeps with me.

He has a pink nose.

Ginger likes cookies

He plays with me everyday.

Mum bathes Ginger everyday.

Ginger eats dog food and drinks milk.

He is scared of cats!

He goes for a walk with dad every morning.

We all love Ginger.

Let's spell new words

dad

mum

brown

food

furry

cats

Ginger

jogs

sleeps

room

pink

nose

bathes

Bats in my hair

My brother is older than me and he has a job delivering morning newspapers before school. Sometimes I go with him on my bike to help deliver the papers.

One morning when we were coming home my brother said, 'Come on, let's take a shortcut through the park.'

Usually, we went down Morgan Street and rode on the footpath to the traffic lights, then turned into our street. Going through the park was quicker but it was winter and it was dark and creepy.

'Okay but don't go too far ahead,' I said.

We rode our bikes through the park. I could see lights shining in the windows of the houses in our street. They didn't look too far away. Anyway, I was with my brother. What could go wrong?

'What's that noise?' Alan said, suddenly. I listened. There were strange sounds in the air on the tops of a few big trees we were heading towards.

There were flapping sounds and cheeping noises. I looked into the dark. The next moment something pulled through my hair. I got such a fright I fell off my bike on to the grass. I shouted out to my brother.

My brother was having a good laugh. 'You should have seen your face! You got such a fright, and then falling off the bike like that!'

It was a bat. The bats lived in the old trees. Bats stay awake at night and now they were on their way back to the trees to sleep. The next time I rode through the park I wore a hat.

The lizard

Belinda was playing in the garden, while mum and dad had coffee under the walnut tree.

Belinda picked up a piece of wood that looked just like a dragon. I was surprised by a sudden movement. 'Don't worry, it's only a lizard,' said dad.

'There it goes!' said Belinda, as the lizard ran towards the porch.

'Lizards like to hide in dark places,' said mum.

Belinda looked for the lizard under an empty flowerpot, but only snails were hiding there. She followed a trail of ants walking along the porch to a stack of firewood. Belinda looked under the wood, but all she found were bugs.

'What about the peach tree?' said mum. 'There are lots of places in the tree for a lizard to hide.' But the only thing Belinda could see in the tree was a spider spinning its web.

Maybe the lizard was hiding under the hedge where it was dark and damp? Belinda looked, but all she saw was a little hedgehog rolled up into a spiky ball.

'Time to come inside, Belinda. We are going to visit grandma,' said dad.

As Belinda followed her dad into her house she turned for one last look . . . and she saw a tiny tail flick under the wood which looked like a dragon. Now she knew where the lizard was.

Down in the grass

Sarah gave me a magnifying glass and said, 'Look at this. Look very closely.'

'What is it?' I said.
'Just look!'
We were both kneeling in the warm grass in our backyard. Sarah gave me the magnifying glass she had been using.

It was wonderful! I could see the tiny insects walking across the muddy surface.

'Can you see the brown ants?' Sarah asked. 'I saw some of them carrying ant eggs and food in their mouths.'

I looked closer. There were other strange insects that were racing about. Without the magnifier I wouldn't have known that this little world was here at all. 'Let's dig into the earth a little bit and see what else we can find,' said Sarah.

Sarah and I spent the rest of that afternoon crawling over the back lawn. Suddenly it was the end of the day and we heard my mother calling us in for dinner.

We went inside to wash our hands and sit at the table for our meal.
'So, what have you been doing all afternoon?' my mother asked. 'You two have been so quiet that I thought that maybe you had gone to another country.'
'Well,' in a way you could say that we had,' said Sarah, smiling. And we told mum all about the magical world we saw through the magnifying lens.

New words

about	flowerpot	moment	sudden
ahead	follow	mouth	suddenly
ant	footpath	move	surprise
bat	fright	movement	tail
before	gave	newspaper	through
brown	good	next	tiny
bug	grass	noise	towards
carry	hair	park	traffic
cheeping	hat	peach	turn
coffee	heading	porch	turn
country	hedge	pull	use
crawl	hedgehog	quick	visit
creepy	help	quiet	walk
damp	hiding	race	walnut
deliver	insect	school	web
dig	inside	shortcut	winter
dragon	job	shout	without
earth	kneel	smile	wonderful
egg	knew	snail	world
face	laugh	sound	wrong
far	lizard	spider	
firewood	magical	spiky	
flapping	magnifier	spinning	
flick	maybe	stack	

What did you learn?

Bats in my hair

What time of the day do they deliver the newspapers?

Why did the boy fall off his bike?

Where did the bats live?

The lizard

What did the piece of wood look like?

Where do lizards like to hide?

Who were the family going to visit?

Down in the grass

What colour are the ants?

What were the ants carrying?

Why did the children go inside at the end of the afternoon?